THE
GILDING
BOOK

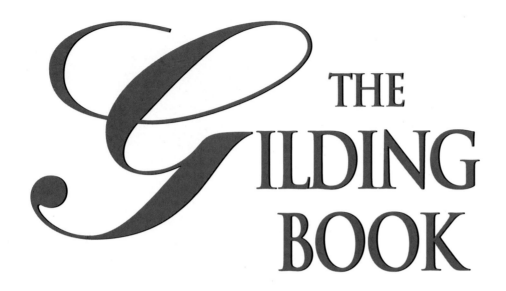

GLENN MᶜDEAN

WATSON-GUPTILL PUBLICATIONS/NEW YORK

First published in 1996 in the United States
by Watson-Guptill Publications,
a division of BPI Communications, Inc.,
1515 Broadway, New York, N.Y. 10036

Copyright © 1996 Tracy Marsh Publications Pty Ltd.

Produced by Tracy Marsh Publications Pty Ltd.
369A Old South Head Road
Bondi, Sydney, NSW 2026, Australia

Library of Congress Cataloging-in-Publication Data
McDean, Glenn.
The gilding book: a complete guide to easy gilding/Glenn McDean.
p.   cm.

ISBN 0-8230-2083-5
1. Gilding. I. Title.
TT380.M39   1996

745.7'5—dc20   96-23152
                                                        CIP

Manufactured in Hong Kong

First printing, 1996

1 2 3 4 5 6 7 8 9 / 04 03 02 01 00 99 98 97 96

PAGE 22

PAGE 26

PAGE 66

PAGE 70

PAGE 46

PAGE 78

PAGE 50

PAGE 58

PAGE 74

PAGE 34

PAGE 30

PAGE 62

PAGE 18

PAGE 54

PAGE 38

PAGE 42

CONTENTS

❧

INTRODUCTION

The sumptuous, soft warmth of gold has made it one of the most sought after metals in history. Such is the fascination and allure of this precious metal that man has tried to simulate its appearance since time eternal. One method has been to beat it into fine wafer thin sheets, called leaf, and apply it to objects which are then polished to a deep sheen, heightening the illusion that the object is actually made of gold.

Some of the earliest evidence of the use of gold leaf dates from about 2300BC, with ancient Egyptian tomb paintings depicting goldsmiths pounding layers of gold into thin sheets. Owing to its intrinsic value and mystical qualities, gold leaf was used to embellish mummy masks, coffins, and funerary items of the Egyptians.

During the Byzantine era, gold leaf was used to decorate and enrich religious paintings and mosaics. In Medieval Europe, gold leaf was used for the illumination of manuscripts, bookbinding, and murals. The furniture of the Baroque period, a time of extravagance and splendor, was frequently adorned with gold leaf, finding particular favor among the affluent. Gilded chairs, tables, and picture frames were coveted not only for their beauty; they were a testimony to the owners' social stature and wealth.

In early years, the craft of the master gilder was kept a closely guarded secret. The apprentice gilder initially served many years sweeping the floor and preparing surfaces. It could take up to ten years to reach the level of gilding proficiency considered necessary to work with gold leaf and eventually he was free to open his own studio.

There are two versions of gilding which have been employed over the years, water and oil gilding. Water gilding is the more traditional, specialist method, requiring meticulous preparation of the surface and a laborious technique of leaf application. In water gilding, the bole, or gilder's red clay, has to be wet in order to activate the mordant before the leaf will adhere. The final step is to burnish the leaf using a special tool called an agate. The agate, shaped like a canine tooth, is rubbed over the gilded surface to increase the smoothness of the gesso beneath and therefore increase the reflective properties of the leaf.

In oil gilding, an oil-based mordant, originally linseed oil, is applied over a coat of bole. These days, the demand for quick results and easy clean-up has led to the use of water-based sizes, though oil-based sizes still make a suitable alternative. Oil gilding does not require such a lengthy process of preparation before applying the leaf, and the leaf is rather easy to apply compared with the water gilding technique.

Much of the mystery surrounding the craft of gilding is probably, in part, attributed to the level of expertise needed to perform water gilding. Today, with modern streamlined methods and products, the work of producing a gilded piece is no longer an arduous one; it simply requires patience and attention to detail. This in no way diminishes the allure and appeal of the master craftsman's work; it merely provides an avenue for the amateur to enjoy what was once an elitist craft. When undertaking the modern version of oil gilding very few and inexpensive tools are required to produce a finished product of high quality and professional appearance.

The inexpensive alternative to gold leaf, Dutch metal leaf, or schlag metal, makes the gilding process economically viable as well. Other metals such as aluminum and copper can also be used for water gilding.

The Gilding Book, with its strong focus on the simplicity of gilding and its extensive list of applications, aims to equip novice gilders with all of the necessary items and knowledge to successfully complete their first project. Once the basics have been mastered, the book offers an array of techniques and paint finishes that can be incorporated into the gilding process to provide stunning decorative items for the home.

The book is compiled in two parts, the first part, from pages 10–17, presents a comprehensive description of the gilding process used throughout the seventeen projects, which make up the second part of the book.

The *Tools & Materials* section offers a photograph of all of the items used throughout the projects plus a brief description of their use.

The *How to Gild* section of the book introduces the different stages of gilding, from preparing the surface to be worked on through to the application of the leaf. *Finishes,* where the seven finishing techniques that have been employed throughout the book are explained, completes the *How To Gild* section. Experimenting with finishes is as much a part of the whole process as the application of the leaf itself. It is recommended that you read these pages carefully to gain a broader knowledge of the entire process and the products used before commencing any of the projects.

The second part of the book presents seventeen projects. Each has been individually designed to provide inspiration on the wide range of surfaces suitable for gilding, as well as ideas on combining other decorative paint finishes with the gilded leaf.

A full color photograph accompanies each project and is intended to provide inspiration on color, design, and use for the completed piece. An introduction provides an insight into the history along with information pertinent to the techniques employed.

Each of the projects have been graded and this information can be found below the introductions. While all the techniques in this book are relatively simple to achieve, it is advisable to start with a project with the *Beginner* grading, until confidence is gained in handling and applying the fragile leaf. *Beginner* projects require no prior gilding experience but you should read the *How to Gild* section first. *Intermediate* projects require some practice of gilding techniques before being undertaken and *Advanced* projects are usually combined with more complicated paint finishes that, with patience, can be successfully completed.

The time taken to complete each project is also noted. The time predicted is representative of working time only and does not include drying time, as this may vary according to climatic conditions.

Following the introductory pages are the step-by-step instructions necessary to complete the project. A strip at the right-hand side of the page shows a close-up of the completed gilded item.

The necessary patterns are located after the projects, beginning on page 86. A Glossary to acquaint readers of terms particular to gilding and a comprehensive list of Suppliers is also included.

The philosophy of *The Gilding Book* is that gilding can be applied to any item or surface, that nothing should be discarded, and that anything can become an object of beauty with the application of gold Dutch metal leaf. Don't be afraid to experiment with gilding — mistakes can often produce the most interesting effects.

TOOLS & MATERIALS

MOLDINGS
Made from plastic or compound materials and are adhered to surfaces with fast-drying glue.

MINERAL TURPENTINE
Used to thin oil-based paints and clean oil-based products from brushes.

SIZE
Either water- or oil-based mordant used to adhere the leaf.

GELATINE
Edible gelatine granules are mixed with water to create a mordant suitable for gilding on fruit or glass.

WHITE SPIRIT
Used to distress and clean surfaces and is added to shellac flakes to create what is referred to as shellac or French Polish.

SHELLAC FLAKES
The flakes are mixed with white spirit to create a resin sealer.

ANTIQUE MEDIUM
Brown acrylic or oil-based paint can be used as an antiquing medium.

SEA SPONGE
The tortoiseshell effect requires the use of a sea sponge.

SANDPAPER & STEEL WOOL
Different grades of sandpaper are used through-out the gilding process, from the first sanding of the raw piece through to final distressing. Fine steel wool (000 or 0000) is used to distress completed surfaces.

STENCIL BOARD & CRAFT KNIFE
Stencils are cut from firm board using a sharp blade.

FURNITURE WAX
Applied to the gilded surface and then polished to a final sheen.

COTTON GLOVES & TALCUM POWDER
Wear cotton gloves, or liberally apply talcum powder over your hands, to protect the leaf from oils and acids that will cause it to tarnish.

GRAPHITE & TRACING PAPER
Patterns are traced from the pattern pages and then transferred to the pieces to be decorated, using the graphite paper.

BRUSHES
Good quality brushes are necessary for the different stages of gilding. Basecoating brushes are needed for the bole, soft-bristled for tamping the leaf and stenciling brushes are required for stenciling.

SOFT CLOTH
Use a soft cloth to wipe dust and sanding from surfaces before applying a sealer or bole. Also used in the antiquing and wash process to wipe away paint.

LEAF
Gold-colored leaf is available as gold or Dutch metal and comes in either loose leaved booklets or on backing sheets. Aluminum, silver and variegated leaf are available in the same form.

GESSO
A white primer, many coats of which provide a sheen-like surface on which to gild.

SEALER
Either water- or oil-based, sealer is used to provide a protective coat over the completed gilding. Matt, satin, and gloss are available.

ACRYLIC PAINTS
Acrylic paints are used almost solely, as their fast drying properties make them simpler to handle.

HOW TO GILD

PREPARATION

Gilding often relies on the reflective properties of the surface to which it is applied to provide the luster and appeal that it rightfully demands. If the surface has not been correctly prepared this luster will not be present. Attention to detail, patience, and care should be employed to obtain a high quality finish.

TIMBER

Raw wood should be well sanded and any nails countersunk and covered with wood filler. Joins should be filled and sanded. After sanding apply a coat of sealer and then sand once more lightly.

Alternatively, gesso can be applied to the sanded wood. After a few coats have been applied the gesso is sanded with fine grade sandpaper to provide a smooth satin-sheen finish to work on.

GLASS & VINYL

These surfaces, though perfectly smooth, must be free of all dust, grit, and oil-based residue, such as finger prints. Wipe over with a cloth dampened with white spirit before use.

METAL

Metal surfaces should be cleaned of all residue by rubbing with sandpaper or steel wool, and then wiped over with white spirit. Apply a coat of metal primer to prevent rust and to provide a satisfactory surface to work on.

FAR LEFT: Gesso has been applied to the frame to provide an even, smooth surface.

ABOVE & RIGHT: Acrylic bole has been applied to the prepared frame to provide a basecoat. Various colors may be used.

PLASTER & TERRACOTTA

As plaster and terracotta are porous surfaces it is important to seal them with two coats of sealer after thoroughly cleaning with either soap and water or white spirit.

PREVIOUSLY PAINTED OR VARNISHED

Pieces that have been painted already do not always need to have the paint completely removed. A general clean and a light sanding will suffice unless the paint or varnish is thick, uneven, or chipped. In this case, the piece should be thoroughly sanded, or even stripped, and then sealed as you would for wooden surfaces.

BASECOATING

After preparing the surface the first step of gilding is to apply one or two coats of bole. Bole means clay, which was traditionally used to create the paint that was applied beneath the gilded surface. The bole used for modern gilding is generally acrylic paint, which also acts as a satisfactory basecoat.

Red earth is generally the color used as it offers a depth to the gold, and provides warm accents where the leaf has skips. Other colors may also be used; black, blue, and green are quite popular. Green and blue are most commonly found under silver-colored leaf, whereas red and black are generally placed beneath gold-colored leaf. The bole should be applied in smooth even strokes, avoiding brush strokes.

APPLYING SIZE

Size is either a water- or oil-based adhesive used as a mordant to attach leaf to a surface. A water-based size has been used throughout this book as it is easier to handle and clean up, dries quickly, and has a longer tack life.

If you choose to use oil-based size, which is called 12 or 24 hour size, refer to the individual instructions of the product before you use it. This size takes longer to dry sufficiently enough to accept the leaf than does the water-based alternative.

The size is applied over the bole in smooth, even strokes, and puddles and runs must be avoided. As the leaf is wafer thin any aberrations beneath it will be visible in the finished product, marring the effect.

When applying size through stencils (as it is in some of the following projects) the brush should be dipped in the size and then almost all of it wiped off again on a paper towel so that the tip of the brush is only just wet. Apply the size lightly to the stencil areas. It is very easy for the size to bleed under the stencil so take care to have the brush as dry as possible while still able to cover the surface adequately.

The size appears milky white when applied to the surface and as it dries it becomes clear. The size will dry to a 'tacky' consistency. To test that the size is ready to accept the leaf, lightly press your knuckle to the surface; if it 'clicks' when you pull your knuckle away it is ready. Do not test the size by using your finger tips as the imprint of your finger will show through the leaf or will remove the size altogether and the leaf will not adhere to that section.

The size will remain tacky for quite some time, depending on the climatic conditions. However, if it is left for too long it will collect dust and grit and be unsuitable for use. If leaving the size to dry overnight, make sure it is in a dust free, covered position.

Brushes should be cleaned immediately after use with warm soapy water to remove all residue of the adhesive. Oil-based size is made of turpentine, so brushes should be cleaned accordingly.

LEFT & ABOVE: Wet size is milky white and when dry has a shiny appearance.

14

Applying Leaf

Gold-colored leaf is available in genuine gold or Dutch metal (an alloy metal made of 90% copper and 10% zinc). Dutch metal leaf is stronger and cheaper than genuine gold leaf. The methods referred to in this book relate to sheets of Dutch metal interleaved with tissue paper. Loose leaved aluminum leaf is also used.

Wear white cotton gloves when handling the leaf to avoid it tarnishing. If you find gloves unsatisfactory talcum powder can be rubbed over the hands instead. If using talcum powder be sure to reapply regularly as the leaf is very sensitive.

Place the book of leaf close to where it is to be applied. If applying it to small areas, firstly cut the leaf into smaller squares, using sharp scissors. After rubbing talcum powder over your hands, or putting on gloves, gently pick up a sheet of leaf and lay it upon the sized surface. As soon as it touches the size it will adhere. Use a clean, soft-bristled brush to tamp the leaf firmly to the surface. Lay the next sheet of leaf to the surface so it overlaps the previous by at least ⅛" (3mm) and tamp down again. Repeat until the entire surface is covered. The pieces that are brushed away during tamping are called skewings and should be saved for filling skips.

As the leaf is applied aim to minimize the lines, or skips, between each sheet. Overlapping will avoid most, but if any skips do occur, they can be filled in by rubbing skewings over the area.

When applying leaf to raised surfaces, such as moldings, it will break around the shape. Lay a piece over the area and use the soft-bristled brush to tamp the leaf into the crevices. Use skewings from this, or previous projects, to fill in the skips. Of course, not all of the skips need to be covered as glimpses of the bole showing through are part of the appeal of gilding.

Once the leaf application is completed, the entire surface, whether flat or raised, should be gently brushed again to remove any skewings.

There are quite a few suitable finishing techniques (see pages 16–17), the most common being antiquing.

ABOVE & RIGHT: After gilding, antique medium is applied. The most common colors used are brown over gold-colored leaf and black over silver-colored leaf.

FINISHING

Once a piece is gilded the technique chosen to finish it will be decided by what provides the most effective appearance, as well as the most protective. The finishes that are available can provide a myriad of effects and they range from sealing, the simplest, through to paint applications that mimic the patina of natural aging.

Even though sealing can be classified as the simplest finish, you must still tailor it to the individual requirements of each of the completed pieces. Therefore the following details should be regarded with care.

Consider the look you want for your piece as well as how durable the surface will need to be. For example, the Grecian Tray will need about four coats of hard-wearing gloss sealer to provide a surface that will be suitable for use as a serving tray. On the other hand, the oxidized Parterre Urn is enhanced by the fact that it has no finish; indeed the effect is extended by leaving it exposed to the elements.

SEALING

The easiest, and most simple method of finishing a piece, is to apply a coat of water-based polyurethane sealer. Oil-based varnishes are becoming outdated as better quality water-based products are being produced. Water-based sealer dries faster, does not impart a 'yellow' look, and is easier to clean up. Satin and gloss sealer provide the strongest finish. When a completed piece is likely to receive wear, extra coats of sealer should be applied to provide a more durable surface.

ANTIQUING

Give your finished project an aged appearance with the simple application of brown paint. A coat of sealer should be applied first to isolate the leaf from the antiquing process. If you do not apply a sealer the leaf may come off the piece when you remove the excess brown paint. Using a soft brush, and working on a small area at a time, brush brown paint, either acrylic or oil-based, on the piece. Acrylic paint will dry faster than oil-based. Without delay rub the paint from the surface using a soft cloth. Flat surfaces can also be antiqued in the same manner.

WASHES

A wash effect can be imparted to the gilded piece by applying watered-down acrylic paint to the surface, most of which is rubbed off again. The effect is enhanced if the gilded piece is not sealed first, as when the wash paint is rubbed off again it will rub through to the bole beneath the leaf, bringing in another dimension of color. This effect generally provides a lovely soft appeal to the piece and many color combinations can be used. Some suggestions are dark green bole and a wash of light green, or burgundy bole with a wash of cream.

VERDIGRIS

Verdigris refers to the natural effect of years of natural oxidation when copper oxide is broken down and appears as a green-gray colored rust. This aged look can be emulated with paint. Choose a bluish-green acrylic paint and water it down to a milky consistency. Using a decent sized brush, apply the paint to the piece, working in a section at a time. Use a soft cloth to rub most of the paint from the surface, leaving only a residue to resemble the natural oxidation. The piece should be sealed before applying the paint to protect the gilded surface.

DISTRESSING

Distressing can be achieved by rubbing the gilded surface with either fine grade sandpaper, steel wool, or a cloth dampened with white spirit. The degree of distressing is entirely personal, but keep in mind that to correctly emulate natural distressing, it should occur in areas that would typically receive the most wear over years of use. Gradually build up the degree of distressing until you achieve the desired effect; you can always remove more of the paint or gilding but you cannot put it back. White spirit provides the most subtle effect.

OXIDIZING

Oxidation can be achieved with chemicals or with safe products from around the home. Apply an acidic based liquid directly onto the unsealed piece once it is gilded. The product used in the Parterre Urn project was household bleach, but do not limit yourself to this alone; experiment with lemon juice, cola, vinegar, and anything else that is acidic.

Naturally oxidized surfaces should be left unsealed as sealing will alter and prevent the oxidation.

WAXING & POLISHING

Waxing and polishing is suitable for pieces that are aged or have had an artificially aged appearance created. The texture of wax provides a patina that adequately mimics years of polishing.

Once the piece has been sealed after gilding, and an aging effect applied if required, rub furniture wax gently onto the surface and polish with a soft cloth until a sheen is achieved.

Use a soft-bristled brush to apply furniture wax to raised or molded surfaces; use a soft brush, such as a shoe brush, to then polish it to a sheen.

GILDED MEMORIES

Photographs are one of our most treasured possessions as they provide a tangible link to our past. Transform this plain, vinyl photograph album into a work of art by adding decorative moldings and a gilded finish. The elegance of the finished album is such that it demands to be displayed rather than stored in a cupboard. Placed on coffee table, it provides an impressive showcase for your most precious memories.

The flat surfaces of the album make this an ideal project for the novice gilder to begin with. Once the basic skills have been mastered they can then be employed on more elaborate and decorative surfaces, limited only by the gilder's imagination.

When handling the Dutch metal leaf, extra care should be taken to ensure the leaf does not come into contact with your hands as the oils in the skin can cause the leaf to tarnish. The use of white cotton gloves or talcum powder sprinkled onto your hands will prevent this occurring.

Decorative moldings are generally made from synthetic compounds and because of the extensive range available, they are an extremely versatile item for the decorative artist or interior decorator. An individual molding placed in the center of the album can be equally as effective as placing moldings around the edges of the album. Don't limit the use of moldings to this application—use them in other gilding projects such as to embellish frames or terracotta pots.

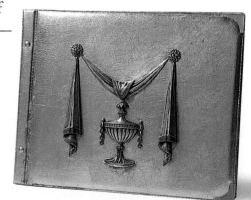

Level of Difficulty
BEGINNER

Time to Complete
2 HOURS

MATERIALS NEEDED

❦

vinyl photograph album

moldings

fast-drying glue

basecoating brush

red earth bole

size

Dutch metal leaf

soft-bristled brush

sealer

brown earth acrylic paint

flat brush

soft cloth

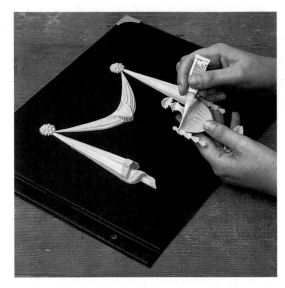

1 If able, remove the pages from the photograph album and set aside. Determine the position of the moldings. Apply fast-drying glue to the rim on the back of the moldings and press into place, holding firmly until the glue has set.

2 Using the basecoating brush, apply red earth bole over the entire surfaces of the album and the moldings. Allow to dry. Apply an even coat of size. The size will change from milky white to transparent and tacky when dry.

The soft-bristled brush is used to smooth the flat areas and to tamp the Dutch metal leaf into the crevices of the moldings.

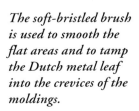

3 Working with the Dutch metal leaf, apply one sheet at a time to the sized surface. Tamp down with the soft-bristled brush. Use the skewings to fill in any skips on the moldings or the flat surface. Apply one coat of sealer and allow to dry.

4 Working on one small area of the moldings at a time, apply brown earth paint with the flat brush. Wipe most off again using the cloth. Gild the back and inside covers of the album following steps 1–3. Apply one coat of sealer.

MOLDED DRAPE

Show off your creative and individual decorative flair by creating this unique drape made from fabric soaked in plaster of Paris. When gilded, the drape can be used to enhance the effect of framed pictures or would create a stunning impact if placed over a plain wall mirror. Try other ideas such as placing the drape over gilded cherubs and hanging them on a feature wall, over a doorway, or above the bed.

The drape in this project is not completely covered in Dutch metal leaf but is left with areas of the red earth bole to show through. To enhance the aged effect, a coat of brown earth acrylic paint is applied to the drape then wiped off with a cloth. As acrylic paint dries quickly, it is best to work on small sections of the piece at a time. Apply the paint to one area then immediately wipe off again. Don't limit yourself to the color of the bole used here; experiment with different colors. A black bole combined with gold and a high gloss sealer provides another look altogether.

The drape can be made in varying lengths and widths. Try embellishing it in other ways such as soaking tassels in plaster and entwining them around the fabric while still wet. A fringed border could look effective if added along the bottom of the drape.

Level of Difficulty
BEGINNER
Time to Complete
2 HOURS

23

MATERIALS NEEDED

❧

acetate

rubber gloves

plaster of Paris

plastic mixing bowl

wooden spoon

79" (2m) of plain
cotton fabric

2 x 8" (20cm) lengths
of thick cord

permanent pen

basecoating brush

red earth bole

size

Dutch metal leaf

soft-bristled brush

sealer

brown earth
acrylic paint

soft cloth

carbon black
acrylic paint

1 Protect the work surface with acetate. Mix the plaster of Paris with water until a creamy consistency is reached. Submerge the fabric and cord in the plaster, squeezing the mix well into the fabric. Squeeze out the excess and remove.

2 Using the permanent pen, draw a guide on the acetate to mold the drape to. This ensures that the fabric will form a drape that is square and straight. Mold the fabric to this shape, creating a swag effect in the center.

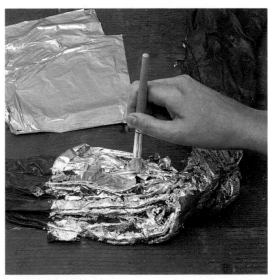

5 Apply a coat of size to the drape. Allow to dry until tacky. Lay a sheet of Dutch metal leaf over the surface, tamping it down into the folds using the soft-bristled brush. Allow areas of the red earth bole to show through.

6 Apply one coat of sealer and allow to dry. Working on small areas at a time, brush brown earth paint over the drape. Using the cloth, wipe most off again. Paint the cords with carbon black paint. Apply a coat of sealer to complete.

3 Wrap a length of cord around one corner of the drape, tucking the ends to the back. Repeat for the other corner. Allow to dry overnight. Glue may be used to adhere the cords if they do not set firmly into place.

4 Using the basecoating brush, apply a coat of red earth bole to the drape. Ensure that the paint is applied to all the surfaces within the folds of the drape. Allow to dry. The painted areas between the folds may take longer to dry.

Brown earth acrylic paint is used to create an excellent and easily achieved aged finish.

MUSICAL CHERUBS

During the 17th century, images of the cherub, a plump, 'heavenly' child with wings, were frequently incorporated into the religious paintings that adorned church ceilings. The cherubs (or more correctly, cherubim) were usually painted blue and were thought to be a symbol of light, knowledge, and heavenly wisdom.

Three hundred years later, the innocent, rosy-faced appeal of the cherub, slightly redefined by 20th century decorating trends, has emerged as a decorative force of its own. No longer only used in paintings or on ceilings, the cherub is now usually seen in the form of small plaster or ceramic statues, featured on the walls or mantel pieces of many homes.

While cherubs are suited to many decorative painting techniques, perhaps it is their rich and long history that makes them particularly suited to the ancient tradition of gilding. These cherubs have been gilded using the contrasting colors of both gold and silver. The entire cherub is firstly gilded with gold Dutch metal leaf then areas such as the fabric and musical instruments are highlighted with silver aluminum leaf. To finish, the cherubs are antiqued using brown earth acrylic paint.

The Dutch metal leaf should be handled as little as possible to maintain the purity of color. Wear cotton gloves or sprinkle talcum powder onto your hands to reduce the risk of skin oils tarnishing the leaf.

Level of Difficulty
BEGINNER

Time to Complete
1½ HOURS

MATERIALS NEEDED

❦

pair of
plaster cherubs

red earth bole

size

Dutch metal leaf

soft-bristled brush

small round brush

teal green bole

aluminum leaf

basecoating brush

sealer

brown earth
acrylic paint

soft cloth

1 Paint the cherub with red earth bole and
allow to dry. Apply a coat of size and allow
to dry until tacky. Apply Dutch metal leaf to the
entire surface and using the soft-bristled brush,
tamp down into all of the crevices.

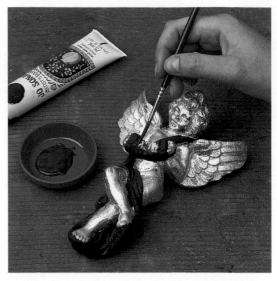

2 Using the small round brush, paint teal
green bole over the areas (fabric and the
instrument) which are to appear silver. Carefully
apply size to the green areas, without overlapping
onto the gold areas. Allow to dry until tacky.

3 Cut the aluminum leaf into small pieces and apply to the sized areas. Use the soft-bristled brush to tamp the leaf into the recesses of the instrument and fabric. Use the skewings to fill in any skips. Repeat for the second cherub.

4 Using the basecoating brush, apply an even coat of sealer to the cherub. Ensure that the sealer is applied to the small crevices, especially around the instrument and fabric. Apply sealer to the second cherub and allow to dry.

The instrument and fabric are carefully coated with teal green bole and size to which the aluminum leaf is adhered.

5 Working on small areas at a time, apply brown earth paint to the cherubs. Before the paint dries, use the cloth to wipe most of it away again, leaving the paint in the crevices. Apply a coat of sealer to both cherubs to complete.

29

GOLDEN FRUIT

Throughout history many cultures have used gilding, not only as a form of decoration, but have incorporated the gold leaf into the food and drink served to celebrate religious or other special occasions.

Use gold leaf to create an elegant, as well as edible, table centerpiece perfect for special-occasion dining by applying the leaf to an array of fruit and nuts. This project differs from the others in the book in that edible gelatine and 24K gold leaf must be used in order for the food to be safe for consumption.

The wax that normally coats the fruit must first be cleaned off by rubbing with a soft cloth and each piece should be at room temperature or the gelatine will not suitably adhere nor dry. The edible gelatine acts as a 'size' to which the gold leaf is adhered.

The fruit used in this project are apples, pears, grapes, passionfruit, pomegranates, tamarillos, strawberries, miniature pineapples, and star fruit.

The rough texture of shelled nuts can also look effective when coated with gold leaf. The outer shell can either be fully covered or brush the gelatine on randomly for a more subtle effect.

Try combining fruit, nuts, and even vegetables to create an eye-catching display, sure to provide a talking point among your guests.

Level of Difficulty
BEGINNER

Time to Complete
1 HOUR

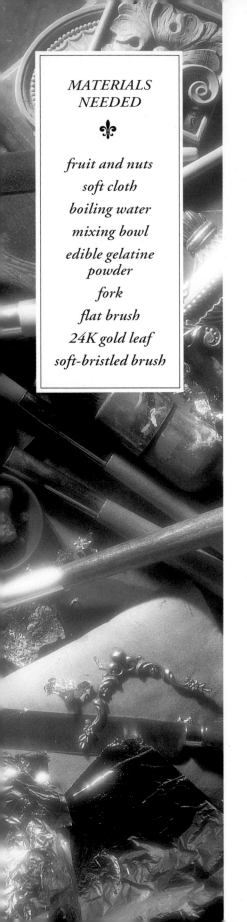

1 Allow the fruit to reach room temperature. If the surface of the fruit is too cold it will resist the edible gelatine 'size' and gold leaf. Using a clean cloth, gently wipe the fruit clean of all moisture and wax.

2 To make the gelatine pour boiling water into a mixing bowl. Following the instructions on the package, sprinkle a small amount of gelatine powder into the boiling water. Mix thoroughly with a fork, ensuring there are no lumps.

A wide range of fruit and nuts, even vegetables, can be gilded.

3 Using the flat brush, apply the gelatine randomly over the surface of the fruit. Vary the application of the gelatine on each of the pieces so they do not resemble each other. Allow the gelatine to dry until tacky.

4 Tear the gold leaf into small pieces and press gently onto the gelatine 'sized' areas. Use the soft-bristled brush to tamp the leaf down, brushing away the excess at the same time. Use the skewings to fill any missed areas.

CANDLE POT

This clever idea of turning a small plant pot into a candle pot combines the earthy textures of terracotta with the rich and warm glow of a gilded finish. The soft enchanting light is further enhanced by gilding the candle itself. A set of two or three makes an ideal number to create a unique table center-piece.

The bole used is aquamarine in color and provides an interesting combination when used with gold. The washed effect is created by applying a white acrylic paint wash over the gilded surface and partially removing it using a soft cloth. The raised areas on the pot are more heavily distressed using this method, allowing the aquamarine bole to show through.

Once gilded, the candle can be further decorated by stenciling a simple design around it. Try placing small pine cones, gilded or ungilded, around the top of the pot and using it as a Christmas table decoration, or grapes and vine leaves as shown here.

There are a myriad of shapes, styles and sizes of terracotta pots available. Oasis (florists') foam and moss are used to fill the pot and can be purchased from most garden shops or florists. Extra pots can be decorated in the same fashion and filled with small indoor plants.

Level of Difficulty
BEGINNER

Time to Complete
1¾ HOURS

1 Using the basecoating brush, apply the aquamarine bole to the pot. Apply size over the bole areas and allow to dry until tacky. Apply the Dutch metal leaf and smooth down over the surface of the pot using the soft-bristled brush.

2 Brush watered-down titanium white paint over the gilded pot using the basecoating brush. Before the paint dries, use the cloth to rub most of the paint off again, leaving it to accumulate over the raised areas on the pot.

5 Working with one sheet at a time, apply the Dutch metal leaf to the sized surface of the candle. Place talcum powder on your hands to prevent the oils tarnishing the leaf. Smooth the leaf down onto the candle.

Use a knife to cut the oasis foam into small blocks and place them inside the pot. Cut a circular shape from the top of the oasis and place it in the bottom of the pot. This will hold the candle upright. Position the candle into the oasis and cover with green moss.

3 Continue rubbing the surface of the pot with the cloth so that areas of the aquamarine bole begin to show through. Rub mainly over the rim and raised areas as these are where most wear would naturally occur.

4 Using the basecoating brush, apply an even coat of size to the surface of the candle, including the top area around the wick. The size will become tacky and change from white to transparent when it has sufficiently dried.

BILLY'S FRAME

During the 17th century, intricately carved and gilt decorated picture frames were synonymous with wealth and were frequently seen in the homes of the upper and middle classes. The craft of gilding and frame making reached a height of popularity in Europe during the 18th century, the elaborately gilded frames becoming as great a component of the beauty of the finished piece as was the painting itself.

Billy's Frame is a modern day interpretation of this centuries old technique. The elaborate and time consuming designs of earlier years have given way to the 90s trend toward more clean and uncluttered lines in interior decorating. The juxtaposition of the silver of the aluminum leaf and the gold of the Dutch metal leaf provides an elegant and interesting finish. The edges of the leaf are blended by simultaneously applying the two different leaves and gently rubbing them onto the surface of the frame. When gilding is completed, the frame is gently distressed by rubbing with steel wool to expose the red earth bole beneath.

Any size or shape frame may be used. The leaf can be applied in a more structured way or try using randomly sized pieces of gold and silver colored leaf to achieve different effects. To provide variety consider using different colored bole, matching the photograph mat board to complement the effect.

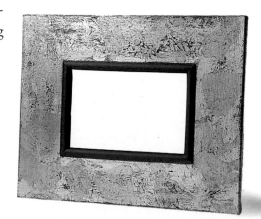

Level of Difficulty
INTERMEDIATE

Time to Complete
2 HOURS

*Continue applying
the Dutch metal
and aluminum leaf
simultaneously to
the surface of
the frame.*

1 Sand the frame and wipe away the dust with the cloth. Apply one coat of sealer and allow to dry. Sand and wipe clean once again. Using the basecoating brush, apply the red earth bole. Once dry, apply a coat of size. Allow to dry until tacky.

2 Rub talcum powder onto your hands. Tear the aluminum and Dutch metal leaf into small pieces. Apply one Dutch metal and one aluminum piece at the same time, overlapping the edges. Rub the leaf down using your fingertips.

3 Once the leaf is applied to the entire frame, use carbon black paint and the small round brush to paint the inner border of the frame. Work carefully, ensuring the black paint does not run into the gilded surface. Apply two coats of black.

4 Using fine sandpaper, gently rub over the sides of the frame. Use the steel wool to gently distress the gilded surface, allowing small areas of the red earth bole to show through. Apply one coat of sealer to finish.

GILDED CHAIR

Gilding as a form of furniture decoration was used extensively during the Baroque, Rococo and Empire periods, imparting a sense of affluence as well as distinction to its owner. As gilding became increasingly popular it was used more as a means of adding interest to the piece, the rich tones of the gold leaf enriching the warmth of wood grain textures.

Today, the move toward more traditional style interiors has led to the revival of gilded pieces of furniture, as well as other decorating accessories.

The intrinsic beauty of the grain of this wooden chair is enhanced using accents of gilded leaf and an attractive stenciled design. Furniture wax applied to the chair and buffed with a soft cloth, provides a soft, mellow finish. To complete the face lift, the cushion can be re-upholstered to co-ordinate the effect.

When handling the Dutch metal leaf, wear cotton gloves or sprinkle talcum powder onto your hands to prevent skin oils tarnishing the leaf.

The gilded chair can be one of several, but as an individual piece it lends a definite sense of opulence and sophistication to any room of the home. Search your home for suitable pieces to gild—an old piece of furniture can easily be given a new lease of life by the addition of leaf.

Level of Difficulty
INTERMEDIATE

Time to Complete
2 HOURS

1 Using the basecoating brush, apply two coats of sealer to the chair. Allow the first coat to dry thoroughly then sand with the fine sandpaper before applying the second coat of sealer. Allow to dry.

2 Apply red earth bole to the areas to be gilded such as the back of the chair, the strip along the front, the small motifs on the back, the legs of the chair, and the balls at the feet. Use the small brush to apply the bole to these detailed areas.

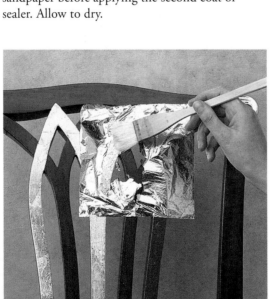

3 Apply an even coat of size to the bole areas and allow to dry until tacky. Using talcum powder on your hands or wearing cotton gloves, apply the Dutch metal leaf to the sized areas. Tamp the leaf down using the soft-bristled brush.

4 Trace the pattern from page 86, and enlarge or decrease to suit using a photocopier. Transfer to the chair. Using carbon black, carefully paint the design. Apply two coats of sealer to the chair. Finish with a coat of furniture wax.

Particular parts of the chair are chosen to be enhanced with gold Dutch metal leaf.

PARTERRE URN

Transform this outdoor fiberglass urn into a stunning interior decorating item by using this simple gilding technique. Once gilded, the urn's aged appearance is achieved by an accelerated process of oxidation. In nature the effects of oxidation mainly appear as rust, though this occurs over a long period of time.

By using products found in the home, natural oxidation can be achieved in as little as 24 hours. Household bleach has been used for this urn, though the acidic compound found in lemons and even cola is a simple and innovative method of achieving a similar result. When products such as these have been used, the piece should not be sealed. To do so would only result in removing the build up of the oxidant. However, if other stonger oxidizing chemicals, such as cupric nitrate, are used it is perfectly safe to seal the item when completed. When using bleach it is important to protect the work area with a sheet of plastic and advisable to wear an apron to avoid bleach splashing onto your clothing.

The completed urn makes a stunning showcase for a large floral arrangement, an indoor planter, or could even be used as an ice bucket. Try placing the urn on a hall table or using it as a table center-piece showing off a fruit or vegetable display. Urns made from substances such as stone, terracotta, or plaster provide equally workable surfaces.

Level of Difficulty
INTERMEDIATE

Time to Complete
1 HOUR

1 Using the basecoating brush, apply one coat of red earth bole to the outside of the urn and allow to dry. Turn the urn upside down to ensure that all surfaces are covered with the red earth bole.

2 Apply an even coat of size over the entire urn and allow to dry. When size dries it changes from a wet, milky white liquid to a clear, tacky finish. Test the size for tackiness by tapping it gently with your knuckle.

3 Apply one sheet of Dutch metal leaf at a time to the sized surface, allowing the sheets to overlap slightly. Using the soft-bristled brush smooth the leaf down, ensuring that it adheres to all of the crevices.

4 Protect the working surface by laying down a plastic sheet. Using a large brush apply the household bleach to the gilded surface of the urn. Leave the urn to allow oxidation to take full effect. This will occur over a period of a few days.

The degree of oxidation depends on the amount of bleach used. This photograph shows the degree of oxidation after being left for only 24 hours.

Starry Cabinet

While the sumptuousness of gold has long been recognized as a means of enhancing traditional style furniture, it is equally suited to modern styles as well. The technique used on this cabinet can be used as a modern interpretation of the use of gilded leaf to add character or to give an old or outdated piece of furniture a fresh, innovative look.

The popular celestial image used is perfectly suited to the shimmering, mystical qualities associated with gold. Adhesive size is applied through a stenciled design and then gold Dutch metal leaf is adhered. When applying size to the stenciled areas, accuracy is essential to ensure clean, crisp lines. Any excess size should be wiped from the brush by blotting onto paper towel. To apply the size to the surface the brush should be held upright and a quick dabbing motion used so that the size does not bleed under the stencil. To complete the cabinet, shellac is used, enhancing the finished look and giving it a slightly antiqued appearance.

Second-hand shops provide a large array of pre-loved furniture, all of which are suitable for this technique. A small table or desk could also look effective if decorated in this manner. Use the gilded star design to create a night sky on a bedroom wall or ceiling, adding a moon design to complete the celestial theme.

Level of Difficulty
INTERMEDIATE

Time to Complete
3 HOURS

1 Using the large basecoating brush, apply two coats of warm white paint to the entire cabinet and allow to dry. Apply one coat of French blue to the front of the bedside table, the drawer and the rim around the top and bottom.

2 Trace the star design from page 86 and transfer to the stencil board in a random manner. Cut out the design and lay it onto the surface. Dip the stencil brush into the size, wipe the excess off onto paper towel and dab it through the stencil.

3 Sprinkle talcum powder generously onto your hands then apply small pieces of the Dutch metal leaf to the sized areas. Use the soft-bristled brush to tamp the leaf down onto the design. Use the brush to gently wipe away the excess.

4 Apply size to the rims of the door and drawer, being careful not to overlap onto the blue or white areas. Allow the size to dry until tacky. Apply Dutch metal leaf to the sized areas, again brushing away the excess.

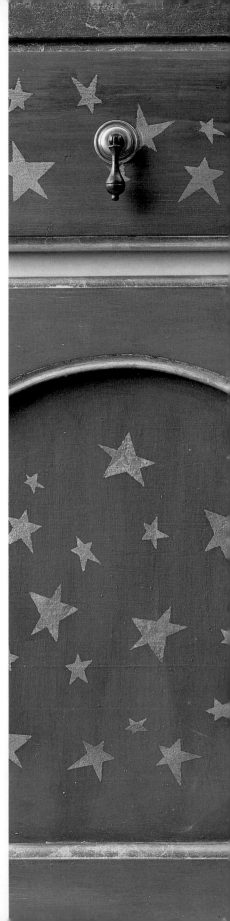

5 Using the large brush, apply two coats of orange shellac to the entire piece. This will antique the piece and prevent the Dutch metal leaf from tarnishing. Allow to dry, sanding lightly before applying the second coat.

The stars are applied randomly over the blue surfaces.

VICTORIAN ORNAMENT

Verdigris refers to the natural effect of years of oxidation when copper oxide is broken down and appears as a green-grey colored rust. The same effect can be readily imitated by the use of acrylic paint. This Victorian garden statue has been gilded, the effect softened and given an old-world charm by the use of an imitation verdigris finish.

The antique green acrylic paint used for this statue closely resembles a verdigris patina and is simply brushed onto the gilded statue. The paint is then partly removed with a cloth, leaving a soft, subdued green hue. Leave more paint on the statue to achieve a stronger degree of 'patination'.

A verdigris finish is a versatile and fashionable method of imitating the effects of weathering and aging and can be used on many surfaces, transforming outdoor objects into striking pieces suitable for interior decorating schemes. Extend the character of the verdigris finish to other surfaces such as terracotta pots, lamp bases, or wooden frames. Objects such as outdoor garden furniture can also be aged in this manner though it is necessary to seal them with two coats of polyurethane sealer to protect the paint finish from the effects of the weather.

Level of Difficulty
INTERMEDIATE

Time to Complete
1 HOUR

1 Apply a coat of sealer to the entire piece and allow to dry. Using the basecoating brush, apply an even coat of red earth bole over the entire piece, ensuring it covers all of the small crevices in the statue. Allow to dry.

2 Apply an even coat of size over the piece. Apply sheets of Dutch metal leaf to the statue. Using the soft-bristled brush, smooth the leaf down, tamping into the crevices. Use the brush to gently wipe away the excess leaf.

3 Before the verdigris finish can be applied to the piece, it must first be sealed. Apply an even coat of sealer to the entire piece, ensuring the sealer is applied into all of the crevices. Allow to dry thoroughly.

4 Using a large brush, apply a thick coat of antique green paint to one small area of the statue at a time. Using a soft cloth, wipe most off again. Allow the paint to remain in the deeper areas of the design.

VICTORIAN ORNAMENT

*Apply the verdigris finish,
completing one small area at
a time, such as the head, then
the arms and bodice, to avoid
any dry lines forming. If
drying occurs, the paint can
be removed by using a cloth
dampened with warm water
or white spirit.*

GRECIAN TRAY

Transform this functional tray into a decorative piece with the application of Dutch metal leaf and a stenciled design.

The harp design is achieved by a two part application. Firstly the stenciled design is painted black and once dry, a random covering of size is applied. Small pieces of aluminum leaf are then gently rubbed onto the sized areas to provide contrast and a more textured look to the design.

When stenciling the design, hold the stencil board firmly in place with your hand. Do not use tape to adhere the stencil to the surface of the tray as it will damage the fragile leaf. As oils from the skin will cause the leaf to tarnish, it is preferable to use cotton gloves or talcum powder when handling the Dutch metal leaf.

The design detail and brilliant luster of the gold are enhanced by the use of two coats of gloss sealer. This high gloss finish is integral to the overall effect of the piece so it is important to ensure that dust particles or brush hairs do not adhere to the surface while it is still wet.

Any size or shape of tray can be used for this project; simply photocopy the design, reproducing it to the desired size. Don't be limited to the use of black for the design; consider deep blue, green, or red, and their effect when combined with gold.

Level of Difficulty
INTERMEDIATE

Time to Complete
3¾ HOURS

MATERIALS NEEDED

⚜

wooden tray

sealer

fine grade
sandpaper

basecoating brush

red earth bole

size

Dutch metal leaf

soft-bristled brush

pencil

tracing paper

stencil board

craft knife

cutting mat

stencil brush

carbon black
acrylic paint

paper towel

aluminum leaf

brown earth
acrylic paint

soft cloth

gloss sealer

1 Basecoat the tray with sealer and sand when dry. Using the basecoating brush, paint red earth bole over the areas to be gilded—the inside base of the tray and the rim. Once dry, apply an even coat of size and allow to dry until tacky.

2 Working with the Dutch metal leaf in sheets, carefully apply them, one at a time, to the sized areas. Smooth down with a soft-bristled brush. Do not handle the leaf any more than necessary or it will tarnish.

5 Allow the design to dry. Reposition the stencil and hold firmly in place. Dip the brush in the size, wiping the excess off on the paper towel. Dab the size over the stenciled areas randomly, partially covering the design.

6 Cut the aluminum leaf into small pieces. Place over the sized areas and gently rub onto the surface. By rubbing on the leaf, the silver areas will have a 'soft' edge, giving a more textured look to the completed design.

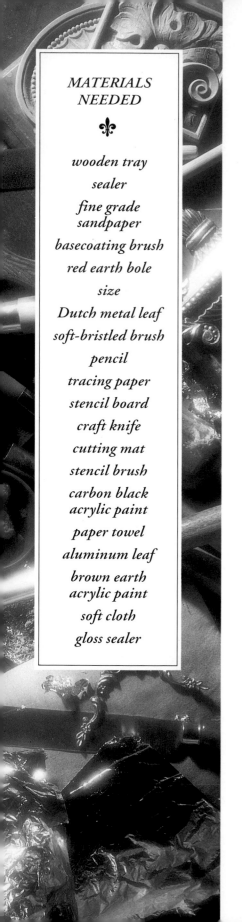

3 Enlarge the design from page 87 to the size required. Trace the design then transfer to the stencil board. Using a sharp craft knife, cut the stencil on a mat or a piece of glass. Turn the stencil as you cut rather than the blade.

4 Place the stencil on the tray, holding firmly in place. Dip the stencil brush in carbon black, wiping the excess off onto paper towel. Stencil the paint on by stippling the paint through the cut stencil, using a quick, dabbing motion.

7 Apply a coat of sealer and allow to dry. To achieve an antiqued effect, apply an even coat of brown earth paint over the inner surface of the tray. Immediately rub most of the paint off again. Antique the rim in the same manner.

8 Paint the remaining areas of the tray such as the sides and the rim along the bottom of the tray using carbon black paint. Allow to dry. Apply two even coats of gloss sealer to the entire tray, allowing to dry between each coat.

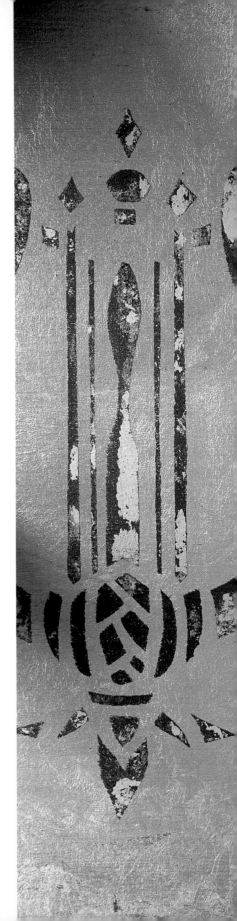

MEDIEVAL ICON

Historically, icons were of a religious nature, the portraits or images usually painted on wood or ivory. The icon was probably most prolific in Eastern Orthodox churches where pictures of Christ, Mary, or the saints were the object of much veneration. Ironically, it was the smoke and incense from devotional candles that caused many of them to be blackened and ruined. While religious icons maintain their popularity today, they now encompass a broader spectrum of images.

Any image is suitable for this project, though the Medieval image used for this icon is complemented by accents of gold Dutch metal leaf. When selecting the board, match it to suit the size of the icon, allowing a border of approximately 3½" (9cm) for the geometric design. The board is covered with plaster of Paris then painted in a contrasting color to facilitate visibility of the carved design. (Blue acrylic paint is used in this project.) Carve down one side of the drawn line, then repeat for the other side of the line, carving the plaster out to the wood to form a shallow 'trough'.

Similar icons can be created by using images found in magazines, old art books or calendars. Match the colors of the geometric border design to complement the overall effect.

Level of Difficulty
INTERMEDIATE

Time to Complete
3½ HOURS

MATERIALS NEEDED

❦

wooden board
plaster of Paris
mixing bowl
wooden spoon
stiff brush
blue acrylic paint
pencil
ruler
craft knife
sealer
basecoating brush
warm white
acrylic paint
flat brush
Turners yellow
acrylic paint
aquamarine
acrylic paint
craft glue
Medieval image
soft cloth
round brush
red earth bole
size
Dutch metal leaf
soft-bristled brush
brown earth
acrylic paint
furniture wax

1 Mix the plaster of Paris to a medium consistency and brush a layer of approximately ⅛" (3mm) onto the board using a stiff brush. Dip the brush into water, and brush it over the surface to smooth the plaster. Allow to dry.

2 Paint the plaster with blue (or any color) acrylic paint. Using a pencil and ruler, draw a geometric pattern, following the main photograph as a guide. Using the craft knife, carve out the drawn pattern.

The drawn lines are carved from a thick layer of plaster of Paris using a craft knife.

3 Apply one coat of sealer and allow to dry. Using the basecoating brush, apply one coat of warm white paint to provide a neutral base color. Using the flat brush, paint the geometric design using Turners yellow and aquamarine.

4 When the design has dried, brush craft glue over the back of the image and press into place on the board. Using the cloth, gently rub over the image, smoothing out any wrinkles or air bubbles that may be trapped beneath the surface.

5 Using the round brush, apply the red earth bole to the areas to be gilded. Apply an even coat of size to the dry bole area. Allow to dry until tacky. Apply the Dutch metal leaf, smoothing down with the soft-bristled brush.

6 Working on small areas at a time, brush a coat of brown earth paint over the surface. Use the cloth to wipe the paint off again. Apply three coats of sealer to the piece. When dry, apply a coat of furniture wax and buff to a soft shine.

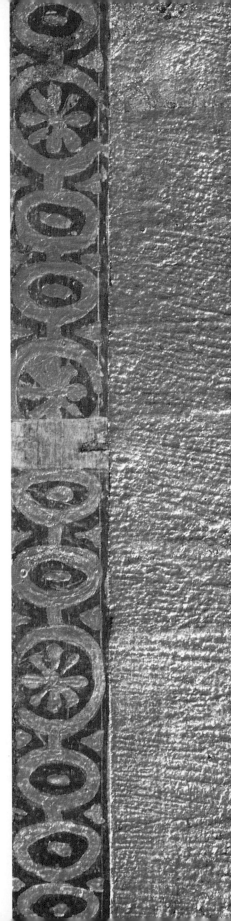

Farm Boy Statue

The art of applying gold Dutch metal leaf does not have to be limited to wooden or plaster surfaces. Metal surfaces, once correctly prepared, will accept leaf in much the same manner as any other surface.

While the brilliant luster of gold has a definite allure, a more mellowed effect is better suited to this metal statue. To simulate the softer patina of weathering and wear, this statue is gilded and then distressed quite heavily.

There are many methods for giving your piece an instant history, one of the simplest being the use of fine steel wool to gently rub the leaf from the statue, exposing the red earth bole and in some areas, the metal underneath. When distressing, consider the areas that would normally be exposed to wear over the years of handling and polishing, such as the folds in the clothing and the prominent areas of the face and skin. To further enhance the aged appearance of the piece, brown acrylic paint is applied then wiped off again, leaving the paint to accumulate in the crevices of the statue.

Enjoy hunting through second-hand shops—you'll be amazed at the huge array of pre-loved items at your disposal. Even objects made of tin, aluminum, or brass are all potentially capable

Level of Difficulty
INTERMEDIATE

Time to Complete
2 HOURS

1 Using the basecoating brush, apply one coat of red earth bole and allow to dry. Apply an even coat of size and allow to dry until tacky. Apply the Dutch metal leaf in small pieces, using the soft-bristled brush to tamp into all crevices.

2 Using the steel wool, gently rub the leaf off the statue, exposing the red bole and in some areas, allowing the metal of the statue to show through. Rub back the areas that would normally be subject to wear.

3 Working on small areas at a time, apply brown earth paint to the statue and while the paint is still wet, use a slightly dampened cloth to rub most off again. Leave the paint to accumulate in the crevices of the statue.

4 Paint the wooden base of the metal statue with carbon black paint. The use of black provides relief and substance to the piece. Using the basecoating brush, apply one coat of sealer to the entire piece. Allow to dry.

The leaf is distressed by gently rubbing with steel wool until the desired effect is achieved.

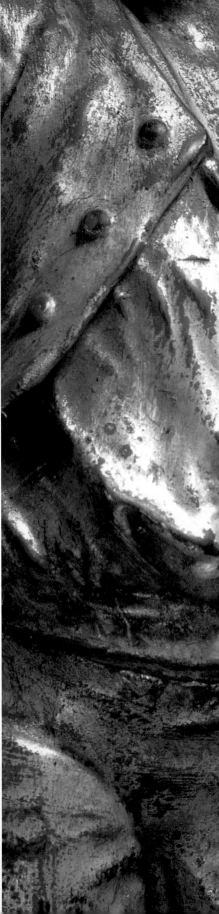

LAPIS LAZULI PLATE

Lapis lazuli is a beautiful blue mineral, flecked with brilliant, shiny spots. In ancient times the Egyptians and Romans incorporated lapis lazuli into their jewelery. The Romans called this stone sapphire, the name now used for the more valuable jewel of a similar color.

In earlier years, lapis lazuli was ground to form the base of the ultramarine pigment used in artists' paints though this is now reproduced by a chemical process.

Recreate the brilliance of lapis lazuli with this simple and unique decorative painting technique. Acrylic paint is brushed generously onto a sheet of plastic film which is then transferred onto the plate. Varying hues of blue are applied in this manner, the layered blue tones resembling the lapis lazuli stone. Small skewings of Dutch metal leaf are rubbed over the surface and the studded rim of the plate is gilded, the combination of deep blue and gold producing a stunning effect.

The back of the plate can be painted using either blue or black. To enhance the detail of the gold and depth of color of the blues, as many as ten coats of gloss sealer are applied to the front of the plate.

The lapis lazuli technique can look effective on a number of surfaces; try it on a vase, frame, or terracotta pot.

Level of Difficulty
ADVANCED

Time to Complete
1½ HOURS

1 Apply one coat of sealer to the entire plate. Using permanent adhesive glue, attach the stud moldings to the plate, positioning them at equal distances around the rim. Apply storm blue paint to the front surface of the plate.

2 Apply Prussian blue onto plastic film then press onto the plate. Rub the plastic film to encourage the paint to transfer to the plate. Using the sea sponge, dab diox purple randomly over the surface. Apply ultramarine using the plastic film.

Match the diox purple, ultramarine, Prussian blue, and storm blue to the swatches above.

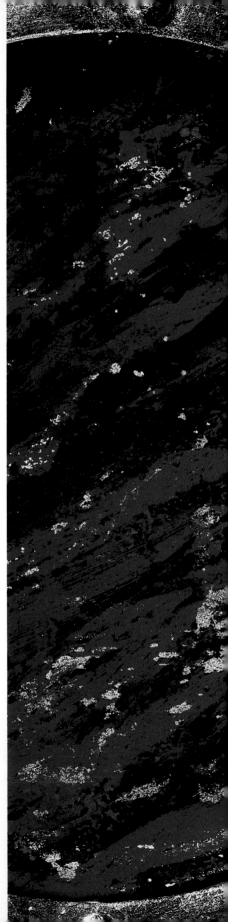

3 Allow to dry. Using the sponge, apply size sparingly to the plate in a random, dabbing motion. Allow to dry. Rub leaf skewings onto the sized areas. If the leaf is too dense, rub with a damp cloth to remove the excess.

4 Re-apply storm blue to the rim, to act as the bole. Carefully apply size to the bole area. Allow to dry until tacky. Apply the Dutch metal leaf, tamping down with the soft-bristled brush. Apply up to ten coats of gloss sealer to complete.

The Dutch metal leaf is applied sparingly to give the appearance of flecks of 'gold' in lapus lazuli stone.

TORTOISESHELL BOX

The beauty of faux painted finishes is their ability to imitate impressive surfaces such as the rich, tawny-brown hues of tortoiseshell. Despite the depth of detail, this handsome tortoiseshell box is deceptively easy to create. To complete the box and to further enhance the warm tones of the tortoiseshell, it is highlighted with gold Dutch metal leaf.

Oil-based gloss polyurethane is tinted with oil-based brown earth paint and then applied to the box, over a Turners yellow basecoat. The tortoiseshell effect is achieved by dabbing a mineral turpentine soaked sponge over the paint, causing areas of the polyurethane to 'break'.

While this is not a complicated process, it is time consuming waiting for each stage to dry. Complete one horizontal surface, or side of the box, and allow it to dry thoroughly before turning the box to begin work on another area. If the box is turned prematurely, the tinted gloss polyurethane will either run or be damaged.

When handling the Dutch metal leaf for this project, it is important to wear cotton gloves or apply talcum powder to the hands to prevent the leaf from tarnishing. When using mineral turpentine, wear rubber gloves to protect the skin.

To finish, the inside of the box can be painted or lined with fabric or felt. Alternatively, turn the box into a safe place for keeping special treasures by attaching decorative gold hinges and a lock.

Level of Difficulty
ADVANCED

Time to Complete
2 HOURS

MATERIALS
NEEDED

❧

wooden box

sealer

fine grade
sandpaper

basecoating brush

Turners yellow
acrylic paint

oil-based gloss
polyurethane

oil-based brown
earth paint

sea sponge

mineral turpentine

red earth bole

size

Dutch metal leaf

soft-bristled brush

To create the tortoise-shell effect, the tinted gloss polyurethane is 'broken' into a random pattern using a sponge soaked in mineral turpentine.

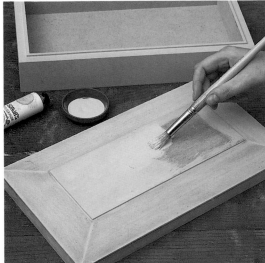

1 Apply one coat of sealer to the box, then sand when dry. Basecoat the areas to receive the tortoiseshell finish, such as the sides of the box and the center area of the lid, with two coats of Turners yellow.

2 Mix gloss polyurethane with oil-based brown paint at a 1:1 ratio. Working on one area at a time, apply the tinted polyurethane using flat, even strokes. Gently dab the tip of the brush over the surface, reducing the visibility of brush strokes.

3 Continue working on the same area. Drench a sea sponge in mineral turpentine, and squeeze out excess. Gently apply the sponge to the wet surface, using a random, dabbing motion. When dry, repeat steps 2–3 for the next area.

4 Apply red earth bole to the unpainted area of the lid. Apply size and allow to dry until tacky. Apply the Dutch metal leaf, smoothing down with a soft-bristled brush. Finish the piece with 3–4 coats of clear gloss polyurethane.

FLEUR-DE-LIS DADO

Fleur-de-lis is a French word meaning "flower of the lily" but is actually thought to represent the stylized form of an iris. Historically, the fleur-de-lis was often seen forming part of the design of heraldic coat of arms.

The simple elegance of the fleur-de-lis makes it a useful design element in many interior decorating schemes. Modern day applications of the fleur-de-lis motif are seen on printed fabrics used for soft furnishings such as cushions and curtains, as well as on wall paper, tapestries, furniture, and synthetic moldings.

Traditionally, the dado rail, a piece of wooden molding running horizontally around the room, was placed at chair height to prevent chair backs from damaging the walls.

When renovating or refurbishing a room such as this one, it is often simplicity of color and design that can achieve the most stunning results. The upper part of the wall was washed with blue, the skirting board was also painted blue, and the base of the wall was under-coated with white. The golden accents applied to the dado and fleur-de-lis design impart a sense of opulence and sophistication.

Level of Difficulty
ADVANCED

Time to Complete
APPROX. 5 HOURS

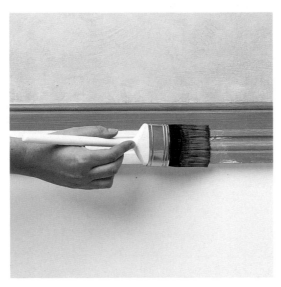

1 Affix the dado molding in a way suited to the wall . The position should be about waist height. Using the large basecoating brush, apply one coat of white paint to the wood dado. Allow to dry then apply a coat of blue paint.

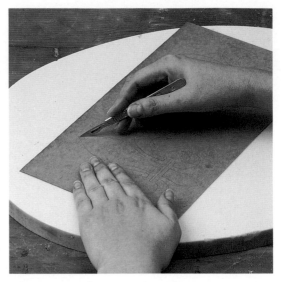

2 Enlarge or reduce the pattern from page 87 to the size required, trace then transfer to the stencil board. Using a sharp craft knife, cut the fleur-de-lis stencil on a mat. Turn the stencil toward you as you cut, rather than the angle of the blade.

5 Using a soft cloth dampened with white spirit, distress the two blue bands of the molding. Gently rub the blue paint back until the white paint beneath begins to show through. Apply a coat of sealer to the entire dado molding.

6 Sprinkle talcum powder onto your hands. Apply the Dutch metal leaf to the sized fleur-de-lis design. Using the soft-bristled brush, tamp the leaf down onto the sized areas. Use the brush to wipe away the excess leaf.

3 Tint the size with a small amount of blue paint. Beginning on the unhinged side of the doorway, apply the tinted size carefully through the cut stencil. Apply the design around the room, finishing behind the door.

4 Apply size to two of the strips along the molding and allow to dry until tacky. Sprinkle talcum powder onto your hands then apply the Dutch metal leaf to the sized areas. Use the soft-bristled brush to remove skewings.

7 To achieve the textured paint applied to the wall beneath the dado molding, sand is added to the paint. Add 1 cup of sand to 1 gallon (4 litres) of ocher paint and mix thoroughly. Test on a board first and add more sand if needed.

8 Using a wide brush, apply the ocher paint and sand mixture to the wall below the dado molding. Apply the paint using large and uneven crisscross strokes. Allow to dry then apply a second coat of paint in the same manner.

VERRE ÉGLOMISÉ PICTURE

Verre églomisé is the application of gold and silver colored leaf to the back of glass or a glass panel, and is enhanced by a painted design. The use of verre églomisé is an ancient one, though it remains popular today, often seen forming elaborate designs above glass doors or incorporated into glass chess boards or tables.

Unlike other projects in this book, two complete layers of both the silver aluminum leaf and gold Dutch metal leaf are necessary to totally cover the design. The leaf is then protected by a coat of black enamel paint which also serves to increase the depth and intensity of the gilded leaf when viewed from the front.

The acrylic size normally used for gilding does not adhere to glass, so it is not suitable for this technique. Instead, a mixture of edible gelatine powder and water will create an adhesive substance which makes an ideal substitute.

When stenciling the design onto the glass, accuracy is essential. Apply the enamel paint through the cut stencil, first wiping the excess paint off onto a paper towel. This ensures that the paint does not bleed under the stencil. The finished design is striking and commands attention when incorporated into any interior decorating scheme.

Level of Difficulty
ADVANCED

Time to Complete
2¾ HOURS

1 Trace the pattern from pages 89–91, enlarging or decreasing the design to suit, and transfer to the stencil board. Using a craft knife, carefully cut the stencil on a mat or piece of glass. Turn the stencil as you cut instead of the blade.

2 Clean the glass with white spirit. Tape the border stencil over the glass. Dip the stencil brush into black enamel paint, wipe off the excess then apply to the stencil. Paint the central stencil in the same manner using black, lilac, and green.

After the black enamel paint is applied, the central design is enhanced using lilac and green.

3 Mix the gelatine powder with water and apply to the back of the glass, working in small areas at a time. Press small squares of aluminum leaf in place and gently brush away the excess. Apply aluminum leaf to the entire outer border.

4 Re-apply a second layer of aluminum leaf over the entire border area to cover any skips. Apply the Dutch metal leaf to the inner area. Apply a second layer. Finish with a coat of black enamel paint to the completed leaf surface.

5 Sand the frame then apply one coat of sealer. When dry, sand again. Paint the entire frame with carbon black paint. Allow to dry. Apply size on the two bands to be gilded. Allow to dry until tacky. Apply the Dutch metal leaf.

6 Apply red earth paint around the inner band of the frame. Allow to dry. Distress the red and black areas by rubbing with a cloth dampened with white spirit. Apply furniture wax to the frame and buff to a shine using a soft cloth.

PATTERNS

The patterns on the following pages are reduced to fit the size of the pages.
They may be enlarged or reduced on a photocopier to fit the pieces to be decorated.

GILDED CHAIR
Transfer this pattern onto a flat area of the chair

STARRY CABINET
The stars are placed randomly over the cabinet surfaces

GRECIAN TRAY
Place in the center of a serving tray

FLEUR-DE-LIS DADO
The fleur-de-lis and circle are
repeated around the room

Cut the edge of the stencil board here and align along the top edge
of the dado rail when applying the size through the stencil

VERRE ÉGLOMISÉ PICTURE – INNER DESIGN
Transfer the inner design to the central area

VERRE ÉGLOMISÉ PICTURE – OUTER DESIGN

Transfer the outer design to the boarder area

The design shown here is split across the double page,
join the two to create the complete pattern.

GLOSSARY

acetate: A thick, rigid piece of plastic used to protect the work surface.

aluminum leaf: A thin sheet of aluminum metal used in gilding.

bole: The colored base beneath the leaf. Can be either acrylic (oil gilding) or a clay mixed with rabbit skin glue (water gilding).

burnish: To polish the leaf by rubbing with an agate tool.

cotton gloves: Used to prevent skin oils from tarnishing the fragile leaf.

distress: To give a finished piece an aged appearance by wearing away sections of the completed surface.

Dutch metal leaf: An alloy of copper and zinc. Also known as Schlag metal or imitation gold leaf. The leaf is available in booklets or in loose sheets.

furniture wax: Applied to the finished piece to protect it and provide an aged appearance.

gelatine: An edible granulated powder mixed with water to create a size for working on glass or fruit.

gesso: White primer made from chalk and used to prepare surfaces.

gold leaf: Can be 22 or 24 carat. More expensive and fragile than Dutch metal leaf.

mineral turpentine: Used to thin oil-based paints and clean oil-based products from brushes.

moldings: Usually made from synthetic compounds and used to embellish surfaces.

mordant: An adhesive.

oil-based gloss polyurethane: Polyurethane varnish used as a sealer.

oil gilding: Af the bole, a size is applyed to adhere the leaf to the surface. The size can be either oil- or water-based.

oxidant: A chemical applied to the leaf causing it to oxidize and appear aged.

patination: A surface finish which provides an aged appearance. The patina can be natural or applied with paint or chemicals.

schlag metal: Another name sometimes used for Dutch metal leaf.

sealer: Used to protect the fragile Dutch metal leaf from tearing or tarnishing. Can also be used for surface preparation.

shellac: A resin used to seal or isolate layers. Orange shellac is used to provide an antiqued appearance, other colors are available. Shellac is purchased in flakes which are then mixed with white spirit to create a liquid.

size: Used in oil gilding to adhere the leaf onto the surface. Is available in oil- and water-based forms.

skewings: Small pieces of leaf brushed away after applying the leaf. These may be used fill in any skips or missed areas on the surface.

skip: A break in the leaf when it is applied to the surface.

stencil board: A firm board especially for cutting stencils.

stippling: Applying the paint in a fine, mottled pattern to gradually build up the depth of color.

tamp: Use a soft-bristled brush to push the leaf onto the surface causing it to adhere to the sized areas and to remove skewings.

verdigris: French word meaning green-gray. Refers to the natural oxidation of copper or can be recreated using a bluish-green paint.

verre églomisé: The ancient Egyptian art of applying leaf to the back of glass.

water gilding: A surface is coated with many layers of gesso and bole. Water is used to activate the mordant in the bole before applying the leaf.

white spirit: Used to clean surfaces, distress or is added to shellac flakes to create what is referred to as either shellac or French Polish.

ABOUT THE AUTHOR

Apprenticed to a leading interior design studio at the age of fourteen,
GLENN M^cDEAN was trained in the art of decorative finishes. He acquired the delicate
skills of manipulating paints and mediums in the finest English tradition, gilding being one
of the master crafts of the time.

Since becoming a master decorator twenty six years ago, Glenn has been commissioned
by a wide variety of clients, his work has featured in restaurants, offices, hotels, and many
homes in Australia and overseas. In 1994, Glenn was the recipient of the Housing
Industries Award for 'The Best Use of Paint', giving official recognition to his talent.

Since opening his own studio, *Trompe & Circumstance*, Glenn has become one of the
most sought after teachers of gilding and paint finishes, traveling and teaching extensively
throughout Australia and overseas.

The Gilding Kit, with its strong focus on the simplicity of gilding and its extensive list
of applications, is the perfect vehicle for Glenn to showcase his impressive range of skills.
By combining various decorative finishes with an array of gilding techniques, Glenn shares
his philosophy that no item should be discarded and that anything can become an object
of beauty with the application of leaf.

Acknowledgments

Thank you to the following companies for supplying props for photography:
Adorabella Tapestries, Petersham, New South Wales; Alexandria McKenzie Interiors, Woollahra, New South Wales; Crystals of The World, Strawberry Hills, New South Wales; Grandma's Craft Shoppe, Huonville, Tasmania; Harlequin Trim, Woollahra, New South Wales; Home and Garden, Sydney, New South Wales; Huon Herbs, Grove, Tasmania; J and T Treasures, Franklin, Tasmania; Menduni Garden Artistry, Summer Hill, New South Wales; Orson & Blake Collectibles, Woollahra, New South Wales; Potter Williams, Ultimo, New South Wales.

Thank you to the following for providing props used in photography:
James Filshie, Rohan Stanley, Regina Walter and Art Gilding, 575—577, King Street, Newtown, New South Wales.

Thank you to The Parterre Garden for allowing access to their shop in Woollahra, New South Wales for photography, including the front cover.

Thank you to Charles Hewitt for allowing access to his studio to shoot the photograph on the inside of the folder and p2.

Thank you to the following companies for providing materials used in the projects:
Art Basics, New South Wales - box on p74, Murdoch & Barclay, Victoria - stud moldings on p44 - Fleur-de-lis moldings on p16–17, Timber Turn, South Australia - plate on p44, Victorian Fair, Victoria - tray on p36

Thank you to Jennifer Bennell of The Painted Finish for her advice during the initial planning of this book.

A special thank you to Chroma Acrylics (New South Wales) Pty Ltd, 17 Mundowi Road, Mt Kuring-gai, New South Wales, (02) 457 9922 for their contribution to the book and support with Jo Sonja's Artists Colors.

Photo Credits – Page 8: Romilly Lockyer/The Image Bank

SUPPLIERS

The following is a list of sources for some of the materials used in the gilding process. These companies sell their products exclusively to art supply, craft, and hobby stores, which are your most reliable sources for gilding supplies. Your local retailer's knowledgeable staff can advise you on your purchases, and will usually order an item for you if they don't have it in stock. If you can't find a store in your area that carries a particular product or will accept a request for an order, or if you need special assistance, the manufacturer will gladly direct you to the retailer nearest you that carries the item, and will try to answer any other questions you might have about its use.

METAL LEAF

Easy Leaf
947 North Cole Avenue
Los Angeles, California 90038
(213) 469-0856
FAX (213) 469-0940

Houston Art & Frame Inc.
10770 Moss Ridge Road
Houston, Texas 77043-1175
(800) 272-3804
FAX (713) 462-1783

Old World Art
1953 South Lake Place
Ontario, California 91761
(909) 947-4928
FAX (909) 923-1185

Reed's Gold Leaf
P.O. Box 160146
Nashville, Tennessee 37216
(615) 865-2666
FAX (615) 865-1903

Sepp Leaf
381 Park Avenue South - Suite 1301
New York, New York 10016
(212) 683-2840
FAX (212) 725-0308

ACRYLIC GOUACHES, MEDIUMS, AND GESSOES

Chroma Acrylics, Inc.
Airport Industrial Park
205 Bucky Drive
Lititz, Pennsylvania 17543
(800) 257-8278
FAX (717) 626-9292
Manufacturer of Jo Sonja's Artists' Colors and Mediums

BRUSHES

Grumbacher
Division of Koh-I-Noor, Inc.
100 North Street
Bloomsbury, New Jersey 08804
(800) 631-7646
fax (908) 479-4285

Loew-Cornell Inc.
563 Chestnut Avenue
Teaneck, New Jersey 07666
(201) 836-7070
FAX (201) 836-8110

Princeton Art and Brush Company
Suite 123 - CN 5256
Princeton, New Jersey 08543
(609) 683-1122
FAX (609) 683-9373

Robert Simmons/Daler-Rowney U.S.A.
2 Corporate Drive
Cranbury, New Jersey 08512-9584
(609) 655-5252
FAX (609) 655-5852

ART AND CRAFT KNIVES

Excel Hobby Blades Corp.
481 Getty Avenue
P.O. Box 1045
Paterson, New Jersey 07503
(201) 278-4000
FAX (201) 278-4343

Hunt Manufacturing Co.
One Commerce Square
2005 Market Street
Philadelphia, Pennsylvania 19103-7085
(215) 656-0300
FAX (215) 656-3700